CH

WOMEN WHO WIN

Cynthia Cooper

Mia Hamm

Martina Hingis

Chamique Holdsclaw

Michelle Kwan

Lisa Leslie

Sheryl Swoopes

Venus & Serena Williams

CHELSEA HOUSE PUBLISHERS

WOMEN WHO WIN

VENUS & SERENA WILLIAMS

Virginia Aronson

Introduction by
HANNAH STORM

CHELSEA HOUSE PUBLISHERS
Philadelphia

Frontis: *Venus (rear) and Serena Williams on the way to victory in their doubles match at the 1999 French Open. Although the sisters have risen to tennis superstardom, their family, their religion, and their education continue to be the biggest priorities in their lives.*

Produced by
21st Century Publishing and Communications, Inc.
New York, New York
http://www.21cpc.com

CHELSEA HOUSE PUBLISHERS

Editor in Chief: Stephen Reginald
Managing Editor: James D. Gallagher
Production Manager: Pamela Loos
Art Director: Sara Davis
Director of Photography: Judy L. Hasday
Senior Production Editor: J. Christopher Higgins
Publishing Coordinator: James McAvoy
Project Editor: Anne Hill

The Chelsea House World Wide Web address is
http://www.chelseahouse.com

First Printing

1 3 5 7 9 8 6 4 2

Library of Congress Cataloging-in-Publication Data

Aronson, Virginia.
  Venus & Serena Williams / Virginia Aronson; introduction by Hannah Storm.
  p. cm. – (Women who win)
  Includes bibliographical references and index.
ISBN 0-7910-5799-2 (hc) — ISBN 0-7910-6158-2 (pbk)
1. Williams, Venus, 1980– —Juvenile literature. 2. Williams, Serena, 1981–
—Juvenile literature. 3. Tennis players—United States—Biography—Juvenile
literature. 4. Afro-American women tennis players—Biography—Juvenile
literature. I. Title: Venus and Serena Williams II. Title. III. Series.

GV994.A1 A76 2000

                                                    00—023019
                                                         CIP
                                                          AC

CONTENTS

WOMEN WHO WIN

Hannah Storm
NBC Studio Host

You go girl! Women's sports are the hottest thing going right now, with the 1900s ending in a big way. When the U.S. team won the 1999 Women's World Cup, it captured the imagination of all sports fans and served as a great inspiration for young girls everywhere to follow their dreams.

That was just the exclamation point on an explosive decade for women's sports—capped off by the Olympic gold medals for the U.S. women in hockey, softball, and basketball. All the excitement created by the U.S. national basketball team helped to launch the Women's National Basketball Association (WNBA), which began play in 1997. The fans embraced the concept, and for the first time, a successful and stable women's professional basketball league was formed.

I was the first ever play-by-play announcer for the WNBA—a big personal challenge. Broadcasting, just like sports, had some areas with limited opportunities for women. There have traditionally not been many play-by-play opportunities for women in sports television, so I had no experience. To tell you the truth, the challenge I faced was a little scary! Sometimes we are all afraid that we might not be up to a certain task. It is not easy to take risks, but unless we push ourselves we will stagnate and not grow.

Here's what happened to me. I had always wanted to do play-by-play earlier in my career, but I had never gotten the opportunity. Not that I was unhappy—I had been given studio hosting assignments that were unprecedented for a woman and my reputation was well established in the business. I was comfortable in my role . . . plus I had just had my first baby. The last thing I needed to do was suddenly tackle a new skill on national television and risk being criticized (not to mention, very stressed out!). Although I had always wanted to do play-by-play, I turned down the assignment twice, before reluctantly agreeing to give it a try. During my hosting stint of the NBA finals that year, I traveled back and forth to WNBA preseason games to practice play-by-play. I was on 11 flights in 14 days to seven different cities! My head was spinning and it was no surprise that I got sick. On the day of the first broadcast, I had to have shots just so I could go on the air without throwing up. I felt terrible and nervous, but

6

I survived my first game. I wasn't very good but gradually, week by week, I got better. By the end of the season, the TV reviews of my work were much better— *USA Today* called me "most improved."

During that 1997 season, I witnessed a lot of exciting basketball moments, from the first historic game to the first championship, won by the Houston Comets. The challenge of doing play-by-play was really exciting and I loved interviewing the women athletes and seeing the fans' enthusiasm. Over one million fans came to the games; my favorite sight was seeing young boys wearing the jerseys of female players—pretty cool. And to think I almost missed out on all of that. It reinforced the importance of taking chances and not being afraid of challenges or criticism. When we have an opportunity to follow our dreams, we need to go for it!

Thankfully, there are now more opportunities than ever for women in sports (and other areas, like broadcasting). We thank women, like those in this series, who have persevered despite lack of opportunities—women who have refused to see their limitations. Remember, women's sports has been around a long time. Way back in 396 B.C. Kyniska, a Spartan princess, won an Olympic chariot race. Of course, women weren't allowed to compete, so she was not allowed to collect her prize in person. At the 1996 Olympic games in Atlanta, Georgia, over 35,600 women competed, almost a third more than in the previous Summer Games. More than 20 new women's events have been added for the Sydney, Australia, Olympics in 2000. Women's collegiate sports continues to grow, spurred by the 1972 landmark legislation Title IX, which states that "no person in the United States shall, on the basis of sex, be excluded from participation in, be denied the benefits of, or be subjected to discrimination under any educational program or activity receiving federal financial assistance." This has set the stage for many more scholarships and opportunities for women, and now we have professional leagues as well. No longer do the most talented basketball players in the country have to go to Europe or Asia to earn a living.

The women in this series did not have as many opportunities as you have today. But they were persistent through all obstacles, both on the court and off. I can tell you that Cynthia Cooper is the strongest woman I know. What is it that makes Cynthia and the rest of the women included in this series so special? They are not afraid to share their struggles and their stories with us. Their willingness to show us their emotions, open their hearts, bare their souls, and let us into their lives is what, in my mind, separates them from their male counterparts. So accept this gift of their remarkable stories and be inspired. Because *you*, too, have what it takes to follow your dreams.

1

"WELCOME TO THE WILLIAMS SHOW"

In 1884, the All England Croquet and Lawn Tennis Club in Wimbledon hosted the first ladies' "lawn tennis" championship. First prize, a lovely silver flower basket, went to 19-year-old Maud Watson. The second-prize winner, who took home a more practical silver-and-glass mirror and hairbrush, was Maud's 26-year-old sister Lilian. Three years later, America held its first championship event for women but, for nearly a century longer, tennis was regarded more as a social event for the upper class than a sport for all to play.

On March 28, 1999, history was about to repeat itself. *Or was it?* For the first time in 115 years, two sisters faced each other across a tennis court in a women's championship final. Teenaged tennis prodigies Venus and Serena Williams had each challenged and overcome some of the top female tennis players in the world in order to elevate sibling rivalry into a world-class, world-watched event at the televised Lipton Championships in Key Biscayne, Florida.

Unlike the Watson sisters, who wore billowy white dresses and, to adhere to the strict social mores of the era, avoided

Tennis fans watch as Venus Williams defeats her sister Serena in the 1999 Lipton Championships. The match marked the first time in 115 years of tennis history that sisters placed first and second in a women's championship final.

sweating by minimizing their athleticism on the courts, the Williams sisters were dressed for action. In their brief, skin-tight, made-for-movement designer sports clothes, both girls could look cool while running hard, each flashing the logo of the sportswear company endorsing her. (Venus, who was 18 at the time, has a multi-million dollar contract with Reebok. Seventeen-year-old Serena has her own endorsement deal with Puma.) The Lipton champ would be bringing home a beautiful crystal bowl and $265,000 in prize money. The second-place sister would also score a crystal bowl plus $132,000—hopefully adequate compensation for losing to one's own sibling in front of an audience of millions.

Although Venus is four inches taller than her "little" sister, both girls are powerfully built and loom larger than life. Venus, at 6' 2", was ranked as No. 6 in the world, and her more compact, extremely muscular sister was No. 16 on the day they squared off at center court in Key Biscayne. With their trademark hairstyle, dancing cornrows brightly beaded in their favorite colors, Venus and Serena Williams did not look like—nor play like—the lawn tennis siblings who preceded them in the spotlight of history. Under the relentless Florida sun, Venus and Serena sweated profusely as they bolted around the court and belted the fuzzy ball at speeds exceeding 100 mph (miles per hour). Both girls can blast the ball at top speeds, matching the blistering serves by the best male tennis champs. In July 1998, Venus had clocked in at 125 mph, the fastest serve in the history of women's tennis.

Further proof that women's tennis is light-years ahead of the lawn tennis played by the Watsons lies in the fact that the Williams sisters

Serena (left) and Venus in their victorious doubles match at the 1999 Australian Open. Both sisters show grace and athleticism on the court, while walloping the ball at amazing speeds.

are African American. Until 1948, when Dr. Reginald Weir became the first African American to play in a tournament in what was then called the United States Lawn Tennis Association, black tennis players were banned from national championship games. In fact, most of the private clubs where such games were played barred entry to all people of color.

Even though superstar Althea Gibson broke through the color barrier in 1949 to become the first black female tennis player competing in the all-white tournaments, the percentage of African-American tennis pros of either sex remains quite small. Zina Garrison, a former world-class tennis player who retired in 1996, says "Good luck" when questioned about the current potential for black tennis players to overcome the racial barriers that continue to exist. "I was ranked No. 4 in the world, and I was still known as the black American tennis player," Garrison explains.

Tennis, in particular women's tennis, has certainly evolved over the course of the 20th century. However, it has a way to go yet before earning top scores for being an equal opportunity sport, one that offers equal pay for both sexes. But the desire to win has not changed and, when Venus glared at her younger sister across the Lipton net, Serena glared right back. "It's complicated enough just to have one champion around the house, but two, that's enough to break up a home," pronounced the girls' father and coach, 56-year-old Richard Williams. "But there's no stopping these girls."

All in the Family

Long before they became known to the world as the unstoppable beaded divas of tennis, Venus and Serena were best friends. And, despite the stresses and strains of mega-fame, the sisters intend to remain best friends.

Unlike many siblings who are close in age, "V" and "Mica" (MEE-kah), as they call each other, have chosen intimacy over cutthroat competition. The two sisters practice together, travel to most tournaments together, and play in doubles events as a team. Off-court, they like to surf, skateboard, and shop the malls together. They help braid each other's hair— which takes at least nine hours to complete and requires around 2,000 beads. The two teens listen to alternative rock music, discuss the cutest players on the guys' side of the pro tennis circuit, giggle over secrets, and comfort and cheer one another. The Williams

girls also worship together, attending weekly services at Kingdom Hall, the church for their faith, Jehovah's Witnesses. "Family comes first, no matter how many times we play each other," Serena has stated. "Nothing will come between me and my sister."

Nothing except a net, sometimes on a widely-watched court at a major Women's Tennis Association (WTA) tournament. The Williams sisters refuse to let their love for one another stop them from playing the game they both love so much, even if they must challenge each other before the rest of the world on their way to the top slot in women's tennis. And there is *only one* No. 1 spot. As their father says, there is no stopping these girls—either of them.

Richard, who splits coaching duties with his

Venus (right) and Serena display their trophies after coming in first and second, respectively, in the 1999 Lipton Championships. Although both are fierce competitors, they remain best friends off the tennis courts.

Richard Williams, Venus and Serena's father and coach, holds up one of a series of messages at the Lipton Championships. While encouraging the sisters' competitive spirit, Williams always puts their education and family commitments before their professional training.

46-year-old wife, Oracene, or "Brandi," is the most famous father in tennis these days. A tall, funny, and wildly outspoken man, Richard is widely respected—and often publicly criticized— for the unorthodox choices he has made in training his two tennis stars. When he first predicted that his girls would one day play each other for the No. 1 spot on the WTA roster, he was scoffed at by experts. Sports analysts belittled Williams for coaching and managing his girls despite his own lack of formal tennis training. The critics also discounted the family's decision to withdraw both girls from the junior circuit, the kids' organized tour of competition, while they were preteens. But Richard Williams knew exactly what he was doing.

By putting his daughters' health and well-being first, ahead of their progress as athletes, Richard has been able to protect his girls from the debilitating physical injuries and psychological troubles that so often sideline young athletes early in their careers. He has also succeeded in helping to build two of the strongest, most confident teens in professional sports. The Williams family's unique coaching technique emphasizes encouragement, having fun, and doing one's best in the most loving environment possible. The sisters receive loads of praise, gentle pointers, and plenty of hugs and kisses while practicing their game. And this "whole person" approach to playing sports has paid off: the Williams girls are healthy, well-balanced, and at the top of their game.

In the crowded stadium at the 1999 Lipton Championships, where he had watched the year before as Venus became the first American-born woman to win the title in a dozen years, Richard scrawled on a hand-held message board with a grease pencil. During the two-hour sister-versus-sister slugfest, in which Venus attempted to retain her hard-won Lipton crown and Serena battled to continue a 16-match unbeaten streak, Richard held up a series of spirited announcements. When the television cameras shared Coach Williams's thoughts with the massive Sunday afternoon viewing audience, his first message was, appropriately, "Welcome to the Williams show." Which sister would prove to be the star of the show was anybody's—and everybody's—guess.

2

"HELLO TO MY FRIENDS IN COMPTON"

During the Venus vs. Serena showdown on the hard courts of Key Biscayne, Richard Williams displayed on his message board what appeared to be a friendly communication to old neighbors in the Los Angeles projects. After bidding "Hello to my mother-in-law, Ora Lee Price," the girls' grandmother, Richard held up a sign that said, "Hello to my friends in Compton." Although the "hello" was simple enough, the underlying meaning of this message was profound and pointed: the Williams family had roots in one of the poorest, most troubled inner-city areas of L.A.

Six months earlier during the most important annual tennis tournament held in America, Richard had recommended the U.S. Open be moved from its spacious new headquarters in Flushing Meadows, New York. Instead of the luxurious Arthur Ashe Stadium, opened in 1997 and named for the legendary African-American tennis player, Richard told the press he thought the world-class event could be relocated to the Williams's hometown. "It's time that a major tournament like this should go to the ghetto," announced Venus and Serena's father and coach.

Venus (right) hugs Serena after defeating her sister at the 1998 Australian Open. By the age of four or five, both girls had shown their natural athletic abilities and love of tennis. They have been inseparable, on and off court, ever since.

In making such vivid public statements, Richard Williams is not trying to be absurdly outrageous. He has long made unpopular choices and unorthodox pronouncements in an inarguably successful attempt to help his family achieve great personal and professional success. And he is continually reminding the rest of the world about the harsh reality that is the life of the poor African-American family, a life the Williamses were able to leave behind.

Hard Labor

Richard Williams was the only son in a family of five children raised by their single mother, who picked cotton to support them. When young Richard helped his mother with her backbreaking labor out in the sun-scorched fields of Louisiana, he learned why she always encouraged him to get a good education. So Richard worked hard to complete high school, earning money for his family at a variety of odd jobs before and after classes. Then he moved west to pursue a college degree in California.

After laboring at a factory in El Segundo, Richard established his own business in the Watts section of Los Angeles, a security guard company called Samson Security. He also started other small businesses, including a phonebook-delivery service. Richard wanted to start a family, too, and he soon fell in love with a nurse he met in church. Her name was Oracene Price. Oracene, a tall, warm, and intelligent woman, was the daughter of an automotive factory worker from Saginaw, Michigan. She was exactly the kind of woman Richard had been looking for: educated, religious, and family-oriented.

Richard and Oracene married in 1972, settling in Long Beach, California. The couple had three daughters in a row: Yetunde, Isha, and Lyndrea. Then, on June 17, 1980, Venus Ebone Starr Williams was born. Fifteen months later, on September 26, 1981, a fifth daughter, Serena Williams, completed the family.

In April 1983, the Williamses moved to Compton, a rough neighborhood of Los Angeles with a reputation for drug problems and street violence. In addition to his security company and phonebook service, Richard established an additional local business, offering low-cost health insurance to his needy neighbors. In his spare time, he carefully studied the game of tennis, viewing instructional videos and reading magazines on the sport.

The tennis obsession had begun after Richard happened to catch a women's tournament on television one afternoon. He became inspired when sports announcer Bud Collins presented the winner with a check for $30,000. "That's what I earn in a year! Let's put our kids in tennis so they can become millionaires," he recalls saying to Oracene.

On the Hard Courts

At their father's request, each of the five Williams girls tried out the game of tennis. Yetunde, who later pursued a medical career and now works in a hospital emergency room, showed talent but lacked interest. Isha, who went on to law school, was also deficient in the intense drive necessary to dedicate herself to the sport. Lyndrea preferred music. But Venus, and later Serena, loved tennis from the very first day.

When Venus was just four-and-a-half years old, Richard drove her to the public tennis courts—two cracked asphalt courts in the heart of gang territory—on the corner of East Compton and Atlantic Boulevards. He had been collecting old tennis balls and, as he tells the story, there were over 500 of them loaded into an old shopping cart in the back of his Volkswagen bus. One by one, Richard tossed the tennis balls to little Venus, who hit them back to her father. Whenever he stopped she would start crying, so he "served" his daughter every single ball, and she hit all 550 of them.

The two went to the East Compton Park tennis courts regularly after that and, a year later, four-year-old Serena began joining them. Both girls had natural athletic talent, the ability to focus for extended periods, and a strong desire to improve and excel. Richard encouraged his two daughters, praising them lavishly and always making sure that they were having fun.

But playing tennis in Compton could be dangerous as well. Richard Williams has written about their gang territory tennis experiences, which he calls "The Myth of Venus, Serena and Richard Williams." The three had become familiar faces at the neighborhood park, where other regulars included future rap stars Easy-E and Snoop Doggy Dogg. One day a gang lieutenant stood up through the sunroof of his car and sprayed the tennis courts with bullets. The Williams girls hit the ground at once, diving for cover. Afterward, Richard advised them not to upset their mother by telling her what had happened. But, as soon as they got home, the excited kids blurted out, "Mama, we got shot at."

"Did my girls get shot at?" Oracene, who was outraged, demanded.

"You know how kids are," Richard responded, attempting to allay his wife's fears.

"They're not joking. I better not catch my kids down there again," ordered Oracene.

As Richard and his wife walked through the East Compton Park neighborhood the next day, however, they saw a policeman chase and roughly capture a local boy. Oracene was upset by the policeman's overbearing behavior and felt that they should intervene. But Richard said no. "Why should we do anything? After all, we ain't coming back to this park," he reminded her.

Oracene understood what Richard was trying to say: Compton was their neighborhood, their home. She took the girls to the park herself the following day.

Serena hugs her father after a match. Although Richard Williams has been criticized for his unusual coaching style, his superstar daughters have developed into well-rounded teens who never forget the importance of their family and their religious faith.

Venus receives a loving pat from her mother, Oracene. The closeness of the Williams family is an important source of encouragement and support for Venus and Serena.

Holding Court

By the time Venus was 10 years old, her father had announced to the press that she would one day be the top-ranked female tennis player in the world, yet her training was markedly different from that of her serious tennis-playing peers. Richard coached his kids himself, limiting their time spent in practice to two-and-a-half hours, three times a week—instead of the customary six or seven hours a day, six days a week.

When Venus was five years old, her father took away her tennis racket for a year because, he explains, she loved the game "too much." Richard consistently emphasized the primary importance of the girls' education and their religion, as well as their devotion to their family. Tennis, Richard taught his two daughters, was only a game.

Yet it was a game the Williams family seemed destined to conquer. From 1989 to 1990, Venus was unbeaten, winning 30 titles in the junior circuit to become the No. 1 player in her own 10-year-old age group as well as No. 1 in the 12-year-old age group. Serena, too, was a preteen champion, winning 46 of the 49 tournaments she had played by the age of nine.

In the fall of 1991, the Williams family moved to Florida. Both Venus and Serena had been awarded full scholarships to attend a Haines City tennis academy for children run by the highly respected tennis coach Rick Macci. The professional tennis instructor was especially impressed with Venus, who he regarded as "a female Michael Jordan" because of her superior strength, agility, and innate athletic skills.

Richard sold his security business, and the family embraced their new life away from the crime-ridden projects and graffiti-covered parks of Compton. But they never forgot their roots. Dubbed by their father "the ghetto Cinderellas," Venus and Serena Williams learned the importance of acknowledging and appreciating where they had come from. After all, they had succeeded in mastering the game of kids' tennis and having a lot of fun on the streets of Los Angeles. Now both girls knew exactly where they were headed: straight to the top of the world tennis rankings.

3

"I Told You So"

One of the seven times Richard Williams held up his message board at the 1999 Lipton final, he was clearly bragging: "I told you so." The message was aimed at all of the tennis experts and sports analysts who had publicly doubted and discredited the Williams family over the years because the choices they made differed so much from the conventional path to success. But from their earliest hours spent on the glass-strewn Compton courts, Richard Williams had impressed upon his two girls that, one day, they would be world champions.

"No one seemed to enjoy our comments, and people were pretty cynical," Venus told *Sports Illustrated* in 1999 about the family's early predictions of their inevitable future domination. "But we're showing that we're capable of doing what we always said we would."

When Venus was only six years old, she already believed that she would one day be the No. 1 player in women's tennis. Her parents had encouraged both girls to play as tough as the boys, to sweat a lot, to run hard, and be the best athletes they could be. Growing up in

Serena, at the net, places a shot as Venus looks on during a doubles match in 1999. The sisters have never seen their race or their gender as obstacles to becoming tennis champions.

the Williams family, Venus and Serena never questioned their right to play sports, to become tennis champions and star athletes, even though they were girls and African Americans. In an era in which one out of three high school girls plays sports, compared to only one in 27 before Title IX (a civil rights statute barring gender discrimination in education signed by President Nixon in 1972) was enacted, the right to smash a tennis ball as hard as the boys do is rarely an issue. But this has not always been the case, especially for black females.

A few decades ago, only a mere handful of African-American women had ever become successful as athletes. Althea Gibson was the sole black female tennis player to achieve fame and some fortune when she won a Wimbledon title in 1957 and, the following year, her first of two U.S. Open trophies. Even in the wake of Gibson's historic progress, only a few African-American women, like Zina Garrison in the 1980s, were able to attain top rankings in professional tennis.

However, these days the field of professional athletics holds more promise for women of color, who have made some headway by the end of the 20th century. The expansion of women's sports at the college level, the introduction of regular television broadcasts of women's athletic events, and the recent surge in popularity of both women's professional basketball and women's soccer has catapulted a number of black female athletes into the spotlight. Unlike the racially restrictive, gender-biased days in which only white male athletes could expect to earn millions of dollars and win over millions of fans, the 1990s proved to be a launching pad for super-talented black women like Venus and Serena.

Althea Gibson, pictured here with her 1957 Wimbledon trophy, was the first African American to win a Wimbledon championship. The following year, she went on to reach the finals of the U.S. Open.

As Richard and Oracene Williams had so prudently instructed their young girls, winning in the game of tennis is no longer just a white man's dream.

Doing It Their Way

In Florida, Venus and Serena spent more hours playing tennis than ever before, running back and forth on the safe, clean courts at Macci's academy, endlessly practicing their serves, volleys, and ground strokes. To Coach Macci's surprise, the girls' father promptly withdrew both sisters from junior circuit competition. With long days focused on tennis, tennis, and more tennis, Richard felt that his daughters needed to pay more attention to their education during their non-tennis hours.

In another unorthodox move, the Williamses withdrew their two youngest girls from public school. The sisters were home-schooled instead, using a variety of hired tutors under the supervision of Oracene and with help from the older Williams daughters. "I made up my mind to stay home and teach my kids," Oracene once explained about their unusual decision regarding the girls' education. "You find people won't do your kids like you want them to. . . . What's good for us is what we know, because we run this family." The Williamses also eventually returned to coaching the girls themselves.

On her own time, Venus liked to study videotapes of tournaments featuring John McEnroe, one of her all-time favorite tennis players. She liked the in-your-face, aggressive style employed by one of history's most talented, and biggest tantrum-throwing players. In 1981, when he was barely out of his teens, McEnroe was branded "Super Brat" by the press after a tempestuous display during the Wimbledon championships.

Perhaps not coincidentally, McEnroe has a younger brother who is also a tennis champ, and their sibling rivalry was once widely celebrated by the media. During the 1980s, Patrick McEnroe was always exceedingly careful not to show excess emotion on the court, lest he be accused of acting as immature as his temperamental superstar brother. But when Serena watched the tennis videos with Venus, she too began to idolize the very verbal and assertive elder brother, who was also known for his obsessive drive to win every point. While the Williamses were in their early teens, however,

Serena seemed destined to follow in the younger brother's footsteps, serving as the quieter, less visible, largely overshadowed sibling.

Between the ages of 10 and 14, Venus did not score any tournament wins. She steadily practiced her game while keeping up with her schoolwork. It was during this relatively dormant time, however, that Venus's fame started to grow. Once she appeared on the front page of the *New York Times,* in *Sports Illustrated,* and on national television, tennis fans began to take notice of the powerful young black girl who did not fit the stereotype for the all-American tennis celebrity.

The McEnroe brothers, Patrick (left) and John, met at their first championship match in 1991. Their sibling rivalry was the talk of the tennis world in the 1980s. The Williams sisters learned the same in-your-face style of play, but unlike the McEnroes, Venus and Serena never let fame get in the way of their relationship.

But few believed that she would rank in the Top 10 before her teens were finished, along with her then virtually unknown sister.

Turning Pro

In 1994, Venus was the most widely recognized young tennis player who had yet to play in a major tournament. Faced with a new WTA rule that would restrict the number of tournaments for players under the age of 18, 14-year-old Venus was anxious to avoid limitations on her choices. She already had enough rules and regulations coming from her own extra-cautious family. So Venus embarked on the difficult process of convincing her parents that it was time for her to turn professional before the new ruling went into effect in 1995.

Richard was not in favor of the idea of his lanky, 6' tall teenager turning pro. Although turning pro would mean that his daughter could begin to earn some serious money by winning at pro events, Richard was concerned about the potential for serious damage to Venus's rapidly developing body. And he wanted to continue to ensure that both of his girls avoided burnout, an all-too-common hazard on the pro tour, especially for young girls.

In competing professionally against the world's top-ranked tennis aces, young players must be able to deal with the intense psychological stress of coming face-to-face with the international press and massive crowds of outspoken fans while battling with the best to climb up the WTA rankings. It is all too easy to crumple before the critical eyes of the world, both physically and emotionally. The history of professional tennis is littered with sad stories of young players who developed career-ending injuries, drug addictions, or severe psychiatric problems due to the body- and soul-shattering pressure of becoming a world champion.

Tracy Austin has spoken publicly about the difficulties she faced as a teenaged superstar, who first got caught in the harsh limelight at Wimbledon in 1977 when she was only 14 years old. At just 4' 11" and under 90 pounds, the determined little dynamo with pigtails wowed world audiences, but she suffered from extreme shyness. "They said my mom tried to make me look like a little girl," Tracy has recalled of her physical injuries and stress-plagued teens. "But I *was* a little girl. I didn't mature quickly, physically or emotionally. . . . I found the press could be very hard. They asked me questions I had never thought about."

Pam Shriver, who is a friend of the Williams family, turned pro at 15 and, the following year, made it all the way to the finals of the 1978 U.S. Open. The next day, the gangly six-footer, an overnight celebrity, was forced to adjust to returning to her high school classes. Pam's career was soon stymied by chronic injuries. She eventually told the press, "Now I know why it happened. I was a tall, skinny kid. I was a weak child and I served too hard for my strength."

Richard Williams was well aware of the common life- and career-damaging problems afflicting top teen pro tennis players like Tracy, Pam, and numerous others. He also recognized the fact that too many ambitious young athletes completely abandon their education in favor of full-time touring and obsessive practicing. So Venus's wise and wary coach continued to veto her increasingly desperate pleas to turn pro.

When the Williams family finally decided to be democratic about the issue and take a vote on whether or not it was time for Venus to enter the world of professional tennis, Richard withheld his vote. So Venus went pro, with the understanding that she had to continue to keep up with her studies and maintain the A average she was earning at the private school in which she had recently enrolled.

Although initially very concerned about her determined daughter's choice to become a pro tennis player at age 14, Oracene realized that it would be pointless to worry about it. Instead, she encouraged the rest of the family to rally around Venus, providing her with the extra love and emotional support she needed to face the demands and challenges of life on the professional circuit.

Everyone in the Williams family had become quite skilled in the art of balancing home and family with the WTA tour when, the next year, Serena made the same choice and turned pro at age 14. By this time the new, restrictive ruling was in effect, but Richard threatened to sue the WTA if it ever refused to allow his youngest daughter to play in a pro tournament. Once again, Richard Williams was making a point, this time airing his belief that the family should be responsible for all important decisions in the careers of their young athletes.

On the Circuit

Before her first pro tournament, the Bank of the West Classic held in Oakland, California, on October 31, 1994, Venus accompanied her family on a mini-vacation. Instead of spending her days practicing compulsively and worrying obsessively about her pro debut, Venus was able to relax and have some fun in Tampa, Florida, at Busch Gardens, a theme park full of amusement rides and wild animals.

When the Williamses arrived in Oakland, Venus still did not have time to fret on the practice courts. She was scheduled to speak to inner-city children, appearing as a teen role model who advised the awestruck kids to study hard, play sports, and pursue their dreams instead of falling prey to the dangerous lure of drugs and gangs.

In her first professional match, Venus demonstrated her powerful serve and amazing athletic skills, winning easily before an enthusiastic audience. Although she did not take home the Oakland tournament title, Venus was pleased with her debut performance and thrilled with the experience of being a professional player. She signed autographs for all the excited fans who flocked onto the court, thanking them for helping to make her first pro event "so much fun."

Most pros play an average of 14 tournaments each year. At age 15, Venus played in only five. She was busy with the rest of her life. She studied hard for her A grades, played her guitar, went to the beach, and worked on clothing designs. Despite her lack of experience on the pro circuit, Venus had been chosen to represent Reebok sportswear as a model and spokesperson. Since she was totally into clothes and fashion, Venus was eager to sign the contract, enabling her to wear the hippest and latest tennis outfits. The contract also allowed the style-conscious teen to provide input on designs and materials.

The five-year, $12 million contract with Reebok also served to dramatically alter the

Even though Venus played only a limited number of tournaments each year after turning pro, her skills improved steadily and she rose quickly through the ranks. Here Venus shows the aggressive style that boosted her meteoric rise from No. 211 to No. 26 during the 1997 pro tennis season.

Williams family's annual income. They soon moved to a sprawling 10-acre estate in Palm Beach Gardens, Florida, a quietly affluent and woodsy town west of celebrity-studded Palm Beach. Of course, the huge yard had·a tennis court—a hard red-clay court—nestled behind a modest two-story brick home. There were also two small lakes on the lush green property, which the girls could ride around in their rickety golf cart filled with tennis balls, or bike-dive into with their dirt bikes. By choice, the Williamses' lifestyle did not suddenly turn glamorous or glitzy, but they had certainly come a long way from the bullet-marked courts of Compton, California.

Rising and Shining

In 1997, Venus started to sizzle on the pro tennis circuit. By winning some tough matches at an increasing number of professional events, her ranking began to rise. By the time she appeared at the U.S. Open that fall, Venus was ranked No. 66, up from No. 211 at the start of the tennis season.

In the brand new, 23,000-seat Arthur Ashe Stadium, Venus played the best tennis of her pro career, winning match after match to qualify for the finals. For the first time since 1958, when Althea Gibson scored the second of her two U.S. Open trophies, an African-American woman was competing in the championship's title match. "Oh man, this is a dream," Venus told the press. "I worked all my life and here I am. It's not even real."

But it *was* real, and a real jumpstart for her climb to the top of the WTA ranks. Although Venus lost to the then No. 1 female tennis ace in the world, fellow teen Martina Hingis of Switzerland, and did not win the U.S. Open title, she accepted the second-place purse, a check for $350,000, and was now ranked No. 26.

Exhausted and overjoyed, Venus thanked God for her remarkable success. She then thanked the cheering fans, grateful to all for her historic experience at the most important annual tennis event in the country. The budding superstar also expressed her heartfelt gratitude to her proud father and coach, who remained as confident as ever that Venus would soon be No. 1 and that Serena also was on her way to the top of the tennis world.

4

"Go, Serena, Go!"

In November 1995, when Serena Williams played in her first professional tennis match, an obscure tournament in Canada, she was unranked by the WTA and unnoticed by tennis fans. Two years later in November 1997, Serena entered the Ameritech Cup, a WTA tournament in Chicago, ranked No. 304. She was 16 years old, powerful and confident, and ready to show the rest of the world her skill on the court.

Pam Shriver had spent a long weekend training with Serena and Venus, and she was awed by the younger sister's incredible strength. "Serena's forehand wasn't big on control," Pam recalled later for *Tennis* magazine, "but as far as power . . . wow! She was just cracking the ball."

In Chicago, Serena also cracked the Top 100, jumping up to No. 96 by beating out two of the highest ranking players, Mary Pierce of France and Monica Seles of America. In doing so, the youngest Williams made history by becoming the lowest-ranked player in WTA tour history to defeat two Top 10 players in the same tournament. "She

---

Showing her power and skills, Serena returns a ball during a match. Following in her sister's footsteps, Serena turned pro at 14. In 1995 she was unranked, but by 1999 she had shot up the ranks to reach a Top 10 position.

hit some great shots," Seles admitted afterward, "and you have to attribute that to her being a great athlete."

Serena has worked extremely hard to develop her game. At 5' 10", she lacks the advantage her sister maintains with her unusual height, which makes it easier for Venus to intimidate and pound balls down at her shorter opponents. "With Venus, everything comes so easy," says the girls' mother. "It's just a natural ability, no matter what it is, athletic or academic. With Serena, it comes a little bit harder, but it makes her work harder, too. She's more of a stick-to-it person."

Sister Act I

At the next big WTA event on her schedule, the Australian Open in early 1998, Serena stuck to it again, winning game after game to qualify for the semifinals. She was able to defeat the No. 2 player in the world, American favorite Lindsay Davenport. Serena was finally beaten by, perhaps, a better player: her sister.

This was their first meeting on the courts of a pro tournament. The Williams sisters had to play their best tennis since they are so familiar with one another's game that there could be few surprises and no secrets. Venus and Serena were the first African-American sisters to compete against each other in a pro event. They made history while they smashed the tennis ball at top speeds, all the while their colorful hair-beads bouncing, spinning, and clacking.

The delighted audience gave both girls a massive round of applause at the end of the match when the two rivals clasped hands and hugged. The thunderous ovation continued as

the Williams sisters turned to face the crowd and, still holding hands, made a theatrical and graceful bow.

"It wasn't fun eliminating my little sister, but I have to be tough," Venus told reporters. "After the match, I said 'I'm sorry I had to take you out.' Since I am older, I have the feeling I should win. I really wouldn't want to lose. But that's the only person I would be happy losing to because I would say, 'Go ahead, Serena. Go ahead, take the title.'"

Serena was equally generous in her public comments about playing against her best friend. "If I had to lose in the second round, there's no one better to lose to than Venus," Serena stated.

Both girls were sure that they would have to face one another again on the pro tour sometime

The Williams sisters acknowledge the crowd's thunderous applause at the 1998 Australian Open. The event marked the first time they had played against each other at a pro tournament.

in the not too distant future. "Serena hates to lose and her reputation is she doesn't lose to anyone twice, so I'm going to be practicing secretly if I want to win the next one," Venus announced to the international press after her win in Australia. Tennis fans and journalists around the world also began to anticipate an equally exciting rematch between the phenomenal Williams sisters.

Despite the accelerating and awesome success both of his teenagers were having on the WTA tour, Richard Williams became increasingly concerned about maintaining balance in his girls' lives. By the fall of 1998, when Venus was ranked No. 5 and Serena had climbed into the top tier at No. 20, their father was preaching to the press, "My girls are very great players, and they'll win lots of tournaments, but I'll tell you what I tell them: Education is much more important."

Even though his daughters had proven themselves to be two of the best female tennis players in the world, the highest ranking African-American sisters in the history of the game, Richard continued to urge his girls to look at the larger picture. As he explained in *Jet* magazine, "Tennis is something to do for a few years, but I'm more interested in what they do with the rest of their lives. They're learning computers and they know that comes first. Last year, I wasn't sure that Venus would play in the U.S. Open until four days before when her computer grades got up to where they should be. This summer, Serena cancelled out of a tournament because she was getting an A-minus in her computer course instead of the A-plus she knows she has to get. You know what I wish? I wish they'd quit tennis and move on to other things."

Oracene agreed with her husband, "I want them to go to college and do other things for themselves," she had told *Newsweek* a few weeks earlier.

Off the Court

Venus, for one, had plans for her future, plans that did not revolve around the WTA tour. At age 18, Venus was seriously considering a career in fashion design. "I'll be asleep or something, and I'll get an idea for a shirt or a dress," she told a reporter during an interview, "so I'll get up and sketch it out."

In fact, tennis was not the only thing on either of the two teens' minds. "There are so many things that I want to do that are more creative," Venus explained. Her sister, who was entering her senior year at the private school from which Venus had just graduated, was fascinated with biology—especially her class's dissection of a fetal pig—and she had visions of becoming a veterinarian.

"Venus and Serena are closer to balanced than any other players in pro tennis," their father had declared in an interview with *Sport* magazine during the summer of 1998. At 18 and almost 17, the two tennis whiz kids were consistently being encouraged by their parents to spend more time pursuing other passions and pastimes in addition to the game of tennis. "Four days a week, we do family activities, bicycle rides, tractor races. They're Jehovah's Witnesses, and they go the Kingdom Hall," Richard revealed in order to illustrate the range of non-tennis interests that capture his famous daughters' off-court attention.

In fact, the Williams family's religion has

long received a significant time commitment from both Venus and Serena. As Jehovah's Witnesses, the girls are active members of a worldwide faith that bases its beliefs on the Bible. Practitioners may attend meetings as often as three times a week in a simple church building called a Kingdom Hall. Witnesses, as they call themselves, dedicate themselves to God, or "Jehovah," studying scripture daily and openly sharing His words with others. Witnesses go door-to-door, distributing reading materials and discussing the lessons of the Bible.

"At first people are a little shocked," Oracene has admitted when asked about the typical reaction at homes where the Williams sisters have rung the doorbell, Witness literature in hand. "They want to talk about tennis, but we'd rather talk about the Bible. . . . We go to rich neighborhoods, poor neighborhoods, everywhere."

For four-and-a-half hours every week, Venus and Serena make home visits and/or write letters, usually to strangers, spreading God's word. Even in the locker room, the girls serve up their religion to anyone who will listen. "People slam doors on us," Serena admits, "but that's their problem. We don't take it personally." Oracene shares the optimistic philosophy that encourages them to continue their sacred work: "They might slam the door this time, but next time it might stay open."

Although Richard does not practice the family religion himself, he strongly supports his wife and daughters in their devotion. The Jehovah's Witness faith forbids lying, gambling, stealing, smoking cigarettes, drinking alcohol, taking illegal drugs, and having sexual relations outside of marriage. Witnesses do not observe Christmas (they believe Jesus Christ was born around October 1), nor do they celebrate their own birthdays. Jehovah's Witnesses also abhor violence, avoiding movies and games that glorify violence, as well as sports that encourage violent play. Venus and Serena do not date, attend parties, or otherwise defy the rules of their religion. After Venus made history at the 1997 U.S. Open, the sisters celebrated with an all-night Monopoly game in their hotel room.

Partly due to their religion, which encourages practitioners to socialize primarily with one another, Venus and Serena have been accused of snubbing their peers, shutting out the other tennis players from their super-tight friendship. But the girls do not allow these or other negative comments to bother them. They have built for themselves an extraordinary private world that only the closest siblings and the best of friends can create. "As long as I'm living, breathing, and winning, I don't care. Let them talk," is how Serena has dismissed all the gossip and criticism that the Williams sisters have received regarding their exclusive relationship. "I really don't want them to have friends outside the family," Richard has stated in support of his daughters, citing cases of well-known tennis prodigies who got into trouble with drugs and peer pressure. "They have each other. That's all they need."

Venus poses in a fashionable off-the-court outfit. In addition to her tennis career, Venus often discusses a future in fashion design or architecture.

Venus (left) and Serena at the 1998 NBA All-Star Jam. The girls share many interests in addition to tennis and socialize together whenever possible.

Eclipsing Venus

When Richard rooted for his youngest child at the 1999 Lipton final, displaying on his sign board the message "Go, Serena, Go!," he was not playing favorites. In fact, the sisters' shrewd coach has long been uniquely adept at speaking to and about each daughter in such equally glowing and exalted terms that neither ever feels slighted. He often points out Venus's unstoppable No. 1 strengths while simultaneously describing exactly why Serena is destined for the top slot in women's tennis. It is a special skill, and one of the reasons why Richard and his two talented girls are regarded with a sense of curious respect by tennis fans worldwide.

"Serena is awesome," Richard told the *New York Times Magazine* early in 1997. "She's going to be better than Venus," he predicted, encouraging his then-unranked daughter on her headlong drive to on-court success. Late that same year, after Serena's world ranking had shot up into the Top 100, Richard reminded the *Times*, "When Venus said she knew her greatest adversary was going to be her sister, she wasn't kidding."

"In my dreams, Serena and I play for No. 1," Venus informed her fans in an interview in 1998. "But since it's my dream, I get the No. 1. Who knows, they eventually may have to co-rank us No. 1. I've always said that Serena is my toughest opponent because she knows my game best. But we're a team no matter what happens on court."

"The better we get, the tougher it gets," Serena added. "We're good players and just have to go at it and do what we can. But I like us being considered a team, because then there's no pressure, no pain on me."

"And then," concluded Venus, "if either of us does well, it's success for both of us."

By the autumn of 1998, the dream of success the Williamses had long been predicting was becoming a reality—for both sisters. Puma had signed Serena to a multi-year, multimillion dollar endorsement contract, and she also had qualified for the U.S. Open. Like her older sister, Serena was also determined to make all of her dreams come true.

5

"IT COULDN'T HAVE
HAPPENED TO A BETTER FAMILY"

A ccording to Serena, her rise in the world tennis rankings came after a fall from a skateboard. In December
1997, Serena was skipping out on a chemistry class in
favor of hanging out on her long, red skateboard when she
wiped out on the sidewalk. As she caught herself with her
left hand, Serena jammed her wrist—*hard.*

"Oh, my, that was terrible," Venus recalled of her sister's
skateboard accident during an interview they conducted
with *Sports Illustrated*, "but what made it worse was when
you [Serena] went out later that day and started hitting in
the rain."

"Yep, and on a clay court," agreed Serena. "That was
mistake number two."

"The session was over, but you said, 'Just let me hit one
more ball,'" continued Venus, intent on recounting the
entire painful ordeal. "Of course, you slipped and fell right
on the wrist. Then you lay there screaming."

But Serena's pain turned out to be her gain. With a sore
left wrist, she was forced to lay off her favorite tennis stroke,
a backhand using both hands, in favor of her weakest

---

*Venus (left) and Serena as doubles partners at the 1999 U.S. Open.
The sisters' aggressive style can intimidate their opponents, but
the girls always seem to be having fun, too.*

stroke, the forehand. After a few weeks of play-ing the game differently while resting her injured wrist, Serena found she had developed a ferocious forehand—just what she needed to improve her game and thrust herself higher up the rankings of women's tennis.

Weak Sister? Not!

A few months later, Serena strutted her stuff at the 1998 Lipton Championships. Known in America as the fifth Grand Slam, Lipton is con-sidered to be a major tennis event, next in importance to the four Grand Slams, the sport's biggest annual tournaments: the Australian Open, held in January or February, followed by the French Open in June, with Wimbledon during the summer, and the U.S. Open in September.

It was Venus who won the coveted Lipton title in 1998, producing serves clocked at 122 mph. Her steaming slammers topped by a dozen miles per hour the tournament's next fastest serve by a woman—Serena was hitting 110 mph serves. After beating out the world's best female tennis player, 17-year-old Martina Hingis, Venus credited her little sister for her advance to the finals. "Serena gave me one pointer that really helped me, which I will not disclose to y'all for fear that it will appear in the papers and over television," Venus told the press, laughing. In losing to Hingis, Serena had learned about the petite Swiss girl's game, while bouncing her own ranking up to No. 31.

The next tournament on her schedule was the 1998 Italian Open in Rome, where Serena battled her way into the quarterfinals, only to face her big sister across the net once again. Venus won the second sister-versus-sister match, but she lost in the finals against Martina Hingis.

When the Williams girls arrived at the world-renowned courts of Wimbledon that summer, Serena was ranked No. 20 and Venus No. 6. After winning several matches, Serena fell hard during a game, straining her calf. Bravely ignoring her injury, the gutsy 16-year-old paired up with Max Mirnyi a few days later to play mixed doubles, in which a male and a female compete against another male-female team. After Mirnyi and Williams handily captured the mixed doubles trophy, Serena crowed to the press, "I am the first Williams sister to win a Wimbledon title. It feels great."

Double Trouble

Whenever Venus and Serena enter women's doubles matches, the sisters always team up. In 1998, the Williams team won their first two WTA tour doubles events, their first win in Oklahoma City, their second in Zurich, Switzerland. With a double dose of McEnroe-style, in-your-face intimidation and aggression on the court, the two sisters held a definite psychological edge over their opponents. And they looked as if they were having a blast at the same time.

When once asked by *Tennis* magazine to describe each other, the sisters appeared to be stumped. Venus gathered her thoughts first: "Serena knows exactly what she wants in life. And if she doesn't know, then I help her to know. She definitely has her mind made up on things. She loves to be confused because of the luxury of being confused. She likes to be out of control because it's fun to be out of control. She likes to amuse herself by playing games and telling jokes. And sometimes she even gets mad at me on the doubles court."

"Venus is very, very tall," was Serena's more concise assessment of her sibling. "Well, Serena's pretty wide," her sister shot back. Then both girls burst out laughing.

In another interview, the sisters compared themselves to their pet dogs, a floppy-eared puppy named Star and Queenie, an elegant Dalmatian. "Star is like me," Serena explained. "She has thick legs and is crazy! Queen is like Venus. She has skinny legs and is a little calmer." (They also own lapdogs, a terrier and a Yorkie named after Pete Sampras.) When asked if they are ever mistaken for each other, Serena has told reporters that such mix-ups, in fact, do occur "pretty often. When we're signing autographs, we'll sometimes say to each other, 'I'll sign your name and you sign mine!'"

These are girls who like to have fun. But the sisters have received some bad press for acting like teenagers, which they are. They have been accused of "headhunting," which is a slang term in tennis for aiming the ball right at an opponent in order to intimidate him or her. They have been taken to task by sports analysts for talking out loud to themselves on the court, for being rude to other players, and for throwing little tantrums. But few reporters have tried to really understand the two tennis superstars, who appear to be rather normal teens, yet who are also so very unusual, different even from their peers on the WTA circuit. Their individuality, like their greatness, sets them apart, and it sets them up as targets for criticism and misinterpretation.

"Sometimes you can have a bad attitude and not set a good example," Venus has said about their behavior both on and off the court.

"We want people to see us, and we know what we want to get across. We want to represent good family values. . . . We make sure that whatever we do is in line with what God would want us to do."

Family friend Pam Shriver defends the girls' behavior, attempting to explain the Williams family's unusual ways to the press and the general public. "They've said time and again that their priorities are family, religion, and education," she says. "People thought it was lip service, but it isn't. Richard has been absolutely determined on those subjects. It's just that they've done it in an untraditional way."

Venus has also gingerly pointed out the impact of race on the Williamses' reputation in

Venus (top left) and Serena sign autographs for their fans. The girls joke about being mistaken for each other and sometimes suggest that they sign each other's names.

the press: "It's not anyone's fault, but people just see black people in a different way, and they can't help it. They don't really understand us. We're a minority in this country. Most people don't grow up around blacks." Most people don't grow up around Jehovah's Witnesses, either. And few people spend enough time around teenaged pro athletes to know what it is like to face the pressure of being the best in the entire world when you are not yet out of puberty.

It cannot be anywhere near as easy as Venus and Serena have been making it look.

Sister Act II

It began to seem as if 1999 would be the year that the Williams family's ridiculed predictions and misunderstood dreams all came true. In February, Serena took home her very first tournament title when she conquered the Paris event, launching what would prove to be a 16-match winning streak. In March, the unstoppable younger sister captured her second WTA event title at Indian Wells in California, and then followed up with five straight wins at the 1999 Lipton Championships. She even defeated her nemesis, No. 1 Martina Hingis, on her way to the Lipton finals.

Venus was having a smashing year, too. She had successfully recaptured her winner's trophy at the 1999 Oklahoma City WTA tournament before power-serving herself back-to-back victories to earn her place in the Lipton Championship finals.

Richard Williams must have been feeling giddy from nervous anticipation when he held up this message on his sign board near the end of his daughters' historic Lipton finals match: "The Williams Family Loves Fox TV." Soon after,

his youngest girl faltered on the court, losing the last two games and the match to her more confident, more experienced older sister. Afterward, Venus abstained from doing her usual happy victory dance, draping an arm around her sister's shoulder and patting it gently instead. Her father's earlier message seemed especially poignant: "It couldn't have happened to a better family."

"I can't necessarily say that our relationship is going to be affected by tennis," Serena later stated to the throng of journalists covering the widely televised and much-discussed event. "We have a strong background. We're Jehovah's Witnesses; we really believe that family comes first."

"In the end, we go home, we live life," her

Serena displays the 1998 Wimbledon mixed doubles trophy with her partner, Max Mirnyi. After their victory, Serena bragged that she was the first Williams sister to win a Wimbledon title.

sister reminded reporters.

In the Williams family, there were no losers that day. Just like her sister, Serena brought home a lovely crystal bowl from Key Biscayne— plus $132,000, lifting her winnings so far in 1999 to close to half a million dollars. Making an exception to his rule banning a clutter of boastful tennis trophies from inside the family home, Richard allowed the beautiful bowl to go on display, announcing, "This trophy will not go in the garage."

The Smash Sisters

Even though the loss to her sister broke Serena's stupendous winning streak, her victories at Lipton elevated her into the ranks of the Top 10 women tennis players. In May, when Serena faced Martina Hingis in the Italian Open quarterfinals, her No. 1 rival was the only player not named Williams who had won more tournaments than she had.

When the press asked Serena if this meant that she and her sister and Martina were now the world's top three players, Serena readily agreed. "Definitely. Of course. The statistics show it. It's just a fact for sure." An exhausted and elated Hingis concurred, admitting, "Beating the whole family all the time, it's not easy," after defeating the younger sister on the clay courts of Rome.

Venus was the next Williams to beat, but Serena's big sister was on a roll. After taking the trophies at Oklahoma City and Lipton, Venus had won her third tournament of the year in Hamburg, Germany, on May 2nd. At the Italian Open a week later, Venus extended her incredible winning streak, overcoming Hingis in the semi-finals, then defeating the imposing, top-ranking

Mary Pierce to win yet another title. "I have a lot of dreams, and most of them come true these days," the victorious Venus told the approving crowd at the Foro Italico in Rome.

By the summer of 1999, Venus was ranked No. 4, her year's purse fatter than ever before with close to $1 million in prize money. With her braces finally removed to reveal a winning smile, Venus was looking as good as she felt as she pounded the ball across the net on her way to the doubles finals in San Diego.

Her partner, Serena, was making the fuzzy ball sizzle, too. Serena's newly braces-free teeth were as dazzling as her superstar sister's. A week later, with a No. 9 ranking and close to three-quarters of a million dollars in her tennis purse following a tournament win at the Acura Classic in Los Angeles, Serena had as much to smile about as her big sister did. After all, the two had taken two more doubles events together in 1999 for a career total of four, more than any sister team in history. And both girls had made history again by becoming the first sisters to simultaneously rank in the Top 10 on the WTA tour. And the season was not even over yet!

The 1999 U.S. Open

At the end of August 1999, Venus served notice that she was well prepared for the upcoming U.S. Open by beating the 1998 title-holder, No. 2 Lindsay Davenport, for the Pilot Pen Championship. The New Haven, Connecticut, tournament provided Venus with her fifth singles title of the year. "I don't get overpowered anymore," the No. 3-ranked Venus announced. "I'm feeling good about playing the big points."

Both of the Williams sisters needed to get the big points in Flushing Meadow, New York, and if they did, there was the chance they would be facing one another across the net in the title match of the 1999 U.S. Open. After Richard Williams boldly predicted that his girls would indeed battle each other in the final game to take home the prestigious trophy, the press turned up the already intense pressure by focusing on the rivalry between No. 1 Martina Hingis and the fast up-and-coming Williams sisters.

Weathering the overblown controversy, Venus and Serena did their best to prove Dad right again. Shrugging off brisk winds, unseasonable chill, and drizzling rain, the smack, sizzle, and slam sisters won match after match, each powering her way to the semifinals.

Serena stunned audiences by dethroning Open champion Lindsay Davenport to secure her place in the title match. Venus, who had made it to the Open finals two years earlier when she was 17, also shocked audiences—by losing to Martina. "I just didn't want that finals to happen, Williams-Williams," Hingis admitted before facing the younger sister for the U.S. Open title.

"Oh, my God, I won, oh my God," an excited Serena gasped, clutching her heart as she became the first African-American woman to win a Grand Slam tournament in over 40 years. This time, it was Serena who scored the biggest points and brought home the biggest purse, capturing the U.S. Open trophy and the Williams sisters' first Grand Slam singles title. "Serena just went out there with a lot of confidence like she's been taught to do all these years," Richard Williams concluded after his youngest made history. "She didn't think she could lose."

Neither sister thought they could lose the U.S.

Open doubles championship, so the Williams family took home that title as well. Venus and Serena, ranked No. 3 and No. 4 respectively as of September 1999, continued to demonstrate that their father has been right all along.

Smart, photogenic, talented, and full of personality, the Williams sisters are besieged by endorsement deals, their garage packed with shiny trophies. Teenaged boys, both black and white, swoon over the attractive, funny, millionaire sisters. But their fairy-tale fame and fortune have not distracted these girls from their real-life priorities. Their family, their religion, and their education continue to keep the two sports stars' perspectives down to earth.

Serena, who recently graduated from high school, plans to pursue an associate's degree in fashion design at a Florida art institute near the family's home. Venus, who takes a variety of courses at the art institute in short, intensive bursts between tournaments, speaks of a future in architecture or fashion, or both. Richard Williams often reminds his celebrity daughters that they are leading a "superficial life," and that "you only get this kind of treatment when you win. People don't care about you when you lose." Both girls have taken that harsh lesson to heart, making lots of non-tennis plans for their futures and living as if there are many more compelling things in this world than the game they play so extraordinarily well.

Serena already speaks French fluently, and she is currently teaching herself to speak Portuguese. Venus continues to enroll in courses in fashion design. "If I'm not enhancing myself," she says, "I feel like I'm wasting my time." The sisters recently purchased a plot of land at a resort community in Palm Beach Gardens,

Serena (left) and Venus sport milk mustaches in this advertisement. Both girls receive many bids for endorsements.

where they plan to one day build a spectacular mansion for themselves. Sometimes they talk of hosting a television show (Serena's idea); other times they discuss opening a clothing store (Venus's idea). "Tennis is a good way to make a million dollars, but they've done that already," the girls' father has said. "They're so brilliant, they'll be great in anything they do. And people won't be asking me if I'm going to be sitting in some stadium watching them play."

The Williams sisters will undoubtedly succeed at whatever they choose to do—and in their own way. "I'll be around for another two or three years to make sure they eat right and practice properly," says Oracene. Richard also intends to advise and supervise the girls until they come of age. When they turn 21, he promises, they will be allowed to map out their tennis careers, make their own endorsement deals—and date. By that time, the whole family predicts that Venus and Serena will be the world's best and highest-ranking female players. "From where we started," their father says, "they're already No. 1."

Tournament Stats (Venus)

(Adapted from COREL WTA TOUR Media Information System)

Year	Date	Event	Prize	Ranking
1994	November 6	Oakland	$5,350	0
1995	August 13	Los Angeles	$1,295	0
	August 20	Canadian Open (Toronto)	$2,175	0
	November 5	Oakland	$10,215	321
1996	March 17	Indian Wells	$1,500	217
	April 14	Amelia Island	$1,285	197
	August 18	Los Angeles	$4,215	192
	August 25	San Diego	$2,600	148
	November 10	Oakland	$3,150	207
1997	March 16	Indian Wells	$20,500	211
	March 30	Lipton	$6,750	110
	April 13	Amelia Island	$2,150	102
	June 8	French Open (Paris)	$14,520	90
	June 22	Eastbourne (Great Britain)	$4,950	79
	July 6	Wimbledon	$7,701	59
	August 3	San Diego	$4,950	64
	August 10	Los Angeles	$4,950	59
	August 17	DuMaurier Open (Toronto)	$2,650	53
	September 7	U.S. Open	$350,000	66
	October 12	Filderstadt (Germany)	$675	26
	October 19	Zurich (Switzerland)	$16,875	26
	November 2	Moscow (Russia)	$16,875	24
	November 16	Philadelphia	$2,600	25
1998	January 18	Sydney (Australia)	$26,500	21
	February 1	Australian Open	$55,667	16
	March 1	*Oklahoma City	$27,000	14
	March 15	Indian Wells	$41,750	12
	March 29	*Lipton	$235,000	11
	May 10	Italian Open (Rome)	$60,000	9
	June 7	French Open	$75,700	7
	June 21	Eastbourne	$2,600	6
	July 5	Wimbledon	$78,961	6
	August 2	Stanford	$36,000	5
	August 9	San Diego	$9,400	5
	September 13	U.S. Open	$200,000	5
	October 4	*Grand Slam Cup (Germany)	$662,400	5
	October 11	Filderstadt	$4,950	5
	October 18	Zurich	$67,500	5
	October 25	Moscow	$36,500	5
1999	January 17	Sydney	$8,000	5
	January 31	Australian Open	$47,402	6

*Won tournament title

February 21	Hannover (Germany)	$40,000	6
February 28	*Oklahoma City	$27,000	5
March 28	*Lipton	$265,000	6
April 11	Amelia Island	$1,800	6
May 2	*Hamburg (Germany)	$80,000	7
May 9	*Italian Open	$150,000	5
June 6	French Open	$38,347	5
July 4	Wimbledon	$75,415	5
July 25	KB Fed Cup	0	4
August 1	Stanford	$40,000	4
August 8	San Diego	$40,000	4
September 10	U.S. Open	$80,000	3

TOURNAMENT STATS (SERENA)

(Adapted from COREL WTA TOUR Media Information System)

Year	Date	Event	Prize	Ranking
1995	November 5	Quebec City (Canada)	$240	0
1997	March 16	Indian Wells	$825	0
	August 10	Los Angeles	$1,375	0
	October 19	Zurich	$1,740	0
	November 2	Moscow	$6,160	448
	November 9	Chicago	$17,850	304
1998	January 18	Sydney	$13,900	96
	February 1	Australian Open	$10,343	53
	March 1	Oklahoma City	$3,600	42
	March 29	Lipton	$29,000	40
	May 10	Italian Open	$14,670	31
	June 7	French Open	$38,769	27
	June 21	Eastbourne	$9,400	22
	July 5	Wimbledon	$22,422	20
	August 16	Los Angeles	$9,400	21
	September 13	U.S. Open	$30,000	20
	October 11	Filderstadt	$9,400	19
1999	January 17	Sydney	$5,450	22
	January 31	Australian Open	$14,575	26
	February 28	*Paris	$80,000	24
	March 14	*Indian Wells	$215,000	21
	March 28	Lipton	$132,000	16
	May 9	Italian Open	$16,000	10
	May 16	German Open	$16,000	11
	June 6	French Open	$20,990	10
	July 25	KB Fed Cup	0	9
	August 15	*Los Angeles	$80,000	9
	September 12	*U.S. Open	$750,000	4

*Won tournament title

CHRONOLOGY

1980   Venus Ebone Starr Williams is born on June 17 in Lynwood, California

1981   Serena "Mica" Williams is born on September 26 in Saginaw, Michigan, her mother's hometown

1983   The Williams family moves to Compton, California

1985   Venus begins playing tennis on neighborhood courts with father, Richard Williams, as coach

1986   Serena begins playing tennis with Venus and Richard

1990   Venus is unbeaten in both the 10- and 12-year-old age groups of the junior circuit

1991   Williams sisters move to Florida to attend Rick Macci's tennis academy; they are withdrawn from the junior circuit

1994   Venus turns pro, playing a limited schedule

1995   Serena turns pro, plays in one tournament on the WTA tour; Reebok signs Venus to a $12 million endorsement deal; Williams family moves to Palm Beach Gardens, Florida

1996   Venus plays in five WTA tournaments, climbs to No. 207

1997   Venus graduates from high school, reaches finals of U.S. Open, and is named WTA Newcomer of the Year

1998   Venus wins first Lipton Championship; clocks fastest serve in the history of women's tennis at 125 mph; ranking jumps from No. 110 to No. 7; Venus and Serena play each other in their first pro match; Serena jumps from No. 453 into the Top 20, wins Wimbledon mixed doubles title with partner Max Mirnyi, and signs a multimillion dollar endorsement deal with Puma

1999   Serena wins first career title in Paris the same week Venus retains her first career title in Oklahoma City; Venus plays Serena to retain her Lipton Championship cup; Serena graduates from high school; Venus and Serena become the first sisters to simultaneously rank in the Top 10 on the WTA world tour; Serena wins the U.S. Open singles title; Venus and Serena win the U.S. Open doubles title

FURTHER READING

Aronson, Virginia. *Venus Williams.* Philadelphia: Chelsea House Publishers, 1999.

Flynn, Gabriel. *Venus and Serena Williams.* Eden Prairie, MN: The Child's World, 2000.

Jenkins, Sally. "Double Trouble," *Women's Sport and Fitness*, November-December, 1998.

King, Billy Jean and Cynthia Starr. *We Have Come a Long Way: The Story of Women's Tennis.* New York: McGraw Hill Book Company, 1988.

Leand, Andrea. "Smash Sisters," *Sports Illustrated for Kids,* August, 1998.

Mewshaw, Michael. *Ladies of the Court.* New York: Crown Publishers, 1993.

Teitelbaum, Michael. *Grand Slam Stars: Martina Hingis and Venus Williams.* New York: Harper Active, 1998.

Watch Tower Bible and Tract Society. *What Does God Require of Us?* (Jehovah's Witnesses brochure). New York: Watch Tower Bible and Tract Society of New York, 1996.

ABOUT THE AUTHOR

VIRGINIA ARONSON is the author of over 20 books. She has written many health education texts and biographies for young people, including Chelsea House's recent GALAXY OF SUPERSTARS title, *Venus Williams*. Ms. Aronson lives with her husband and young son in South Florida, not too far from the Williams family compound.

HANNAH STORM, NBC Sports play-by-play announcer, reporter, and studio host, made her debut in 1992 at Wimbledon during the All England Tennis Championships. Shortly thereafter, she was paired with Jim Lampley to cohost the *Olympic Show* for the 1992 Olympic Games in Barcelona. Later that year, Storm was named cohost of *Notre Dame Saturday*, NBC's college football pregame show. Adding to her repertoire, Storm became a reporter for the 1994 Major League All-Star Game and the pregame host for the 1995, 1997, and 1999 World Series. Storm's success as host of *NBA Showtime* during the 1997-98 season won her the role as studio host for the inaugural season of the Women's National Basketball Association in 1998.

In 1996, Storm was selected as NBC's host for the Summer Olympics in Atlanta, and she has been named as host for both the 2000 Summer Olympics in Sydney and the 2002 Winter Olympics in Salt Lake City. Storm received a Gracie Allen Award for Outstanding Personal Achievement, which was presented by the American Women in Radio and Television Foundation (AWRTF), for her coverage of the 1999 NBA Finals and 1999 World Series. She has been married to NBC Sports broadcaster Dan Hicks since 1994. They have two daughters.

INDEX